PRELUDES

& OTHER POEMS

PRAISE FOR EARL J. WILCOX

"Earl Wilcox writes with heart, but does not wear his heart on a sentimental sleeve; rather he embeds it in craft and artistry developed over— dare I say it—a very long lifetime. And yet it is 'The urge to know what lies / Ahead more than gone before,' as Earl has elsewhere written, that you will find and feel in this book."
—**JAMES PENHA**, *editor, The New Verse News.*

"These poems aren't for a single read—they're to be read, re-read, and feasted upon."
—**GLORIA G. JONES,** PhD, *Emeritus Professor of English & former Dean, Winthrop University.*

"What a beautiful thing Earl has created. I want everyone I know to read these poems."
—**ROB MCDONALD**, *PhD, Professor of English & Associate Dean, Virginia Military Institute; photographer.*

"Like a well-loved chest handed down through time... the scholar's ear is in the cadence, the joy in the expedition."
—**EVELYNE WEEKS**, *Poet & Former Instructor of English, Winthrop University*

PRELUDES
& OTHER POEMS

EARL J. WILCOX

LOBLOLLY PRESS | ASHEVILLE, NC

Published by Loblolly Press

loblollypress.com

Asheville, NC

Designed by Andrew Mack
Instagram: @loblolly_press
Newsletter: loblollypress.substack.com

Paperback ISBN: 979-8-9900730-9-8

Printed in the United States of America

First Printing, November 2025

for Bettye, magnificent spouse

CONTENTS

INTRODUCTION

Earl J. Wilcox's second collection of poetry arrives after a long life in letters. He taught literature for four decades and retired as Professor of English at Winthrop University, where he also received emeritus recognition from the Board of Trustees. He earned his PhD at Vanderbilt University. His editorial and critical record runs deep: co-author of *Roads Not Taken: Rereading Robert Frost*, founding editor of *The Robert Frost Review*, and editor of the Houghton Mifflin Centennial Edition of Jack London's *The Call of the Wild*.

His late-life turn to poetry has been steady and public, with dozens of pieces in *The New Verse News* and other venues, culminating in the publication of a wide-ranging and far-reaching collection of more than 90 poems, his debut, *The Surfacing of Joy*.

That work, of course, was the first title published by Loblolly Press, an endeavor in which Earl can be credited as our main partner. The proceeds of his debut he gifted to the Press with the guidance, "Take this and do for others what we've done for me." Like Earl has done time and time again, even his first act of publishing creative work set waypoints for those that have and will come after him, myself included.

I first met Earl at a family dinner. Soon after, I enrolled in the half-term seminar he co-taught on Robert Penn Warren's *All the King's Men* alongside his longtime colleague, friend, and neighbor Dr. Gloria Jones. At eighty-two he walked in wearing full St. Louis Cardinals gear, stocking cap included, and closed the course 6 weeks later by showing us a letter he'd received from Warren, himself.

After I graduated, I moved north for work, and his emails to me began—poems attached, notes in the margins, more poems. Years of exchange followed. What I did not see at the start I see now:

a body of work taking shape with fidelity to place, to relations, and to story, begun long before Earl came into my life.

This selection advances that record. Its arc has been carefully curated to be seasonal and mortal: onset of winter and taking leave, but also persistence, ritual, and the stubborn act of renewal. The tonal center is plain and not without attention to form or poetic complexity. That center invites certain lineages.

The act of seeing, of holding the world in steady focus, links him to Emily Dickinson, Robert Frost, and T.S. Eliot. In *Hydrangea Light*, the "pink and blue polka dots" that are not real dots at all recall Dickinson's precision—vision turned inward until perception becomes revelation. In *Perspective*, Wilcox extends and reimagines Frost's reasoned cadence and his counsel to "choose something like a star," placing it instead above a Carolina balcony where light is less an escape than a discipline. In *In Winter* and *Felicity*, time becomes both calendar and elegy. The order Eliot sought in liturgy reappears in Wilcox as domestic ritual—lamps, robes, cots, and rain translating the everyday into the sacred:

A worm-tune loops endlessly between my ears,

                Carly Simon's *Let the River Run*. I consider if

       I also hear rain,

                  or do I dream?

The second attention is physical, the life of voice and gesture. *Just So* and *On the Demise of a Pygmy Mouse* carry the compressed wit and form of ee cummings—emotion held tight inside syntax. *Nomenclature* and *Mourning* echo Galway Kinnell's tenderness toward the aging body, the acceptance that naming itself is a form of care.

Finally comes witness, the moral stance of belonging. *Delta Pilgrimage* and *Peace Like a River* move in Robert Penn Warren's register, where what is remembered presses against conscience and grief deepens into story. *Adding Up the Losses* and *Decomposition* broaden that field into Walt Whitman's democratic vision of the sublime, every creature and root given its due. The poems name what is vanishing and what remains, trusting the act of attention to preserve it.

Across all these lines of inheritance, Earl's work keeps faith with the world—seeing clearly, speaking plainly, staying present to its unsteady grace. Here's a poet writing from the steady light of long attention, proving that clarity is its own grace—a long look made luminous.

Music then threads the book. There is a sharp, bitter irony in the hearing and sight that have dimmed for him in recent years, given how often he sings under his breath, quotes a chorus, or lets a poetic line sink into tune. The classroom lecturer still lives in the stanza: a prelude, then the proof.

Two touchstones frame the collection's reach. *Radio Baseball* reconsiders the American father-son myth with an ethic of truth over pose; its permissions are Frost's and Warren's at once, restrained and candid. *Mockingbird, the Morning After* keeps moral witness during grief and asks what song owes to sorrow; its final triad—loss, pain, a weary world—lands without flourish.

Winter, too, threads these pages, not as backdrop but as method. The late poems accept decay and make room for grace. *Mutability* names this plainly: the gray matter "gathers itself for future losses," clears a plot, then "makes room where grace abides." That gesture stands at the book's center, and, I think, at Earl's as well.

My place in this work has shifted over the years—student, reader, mentee, editor, designer, publisher, and, finally, friend. I have edited more than two hundred of Earl's poems, with hundreds more waiting their turn. The work goes on.

What we hold here is not an ending but a harvest, the yield of years of ecstatic, attentive living. With this work, Earl sinks both hands into rich, Carolina soil: *celebrating Spring / deep underneath jagged / fingernails*, showing us how to entomb bulbs in winter— how in spring they unfurl, then bloom.

AM, October 2025

The Poets light but Lamps —
Themselves — go out —
The Wicks they stimulate
If vital Light

Inhere as do the Suns —
Each Age a Lens
Disseminating their
Circumference —

EMILY DICKINSON, *The Poets
light but Lamps — (930)*

The showers beat
On broken blinds and chimney-pots,
And at the corner of the street
A lonely cab-horse steams and stamps.

And then the lighting of the lamps.

T.S. ELIOT, *Preludes*

JUST SO

On slick streets,
        moist from constant showers,
                leaves are stacked in piles like frail pyramids.

Cars swish by, swirling frenzied leaves loose.
        The pyramids remain unmoved.
                Piles have been placed just so. Just so.

FIRST DAY OF FALL

A bright red cup on a white table
Beside a sweet dessert in a blue
Saucer caught together on a Sunday
Afternoon full of sunlight and shade
While swallows and sparrows twitter
Aloft between elms beginning to
Shed their pale pink petals. Yellow
Hydrangeas join the cascading choir
As chimes from the steeple usher
In the afternoon with autumn gladness
Spilling out into every haunt, every hollow.

STUDY OF RED AND WHITE

Winter brained bevy
of yellow-striped bees
await hot summer days
to form hives, mate
deep underneath the
dense rock wall touching
the red lounger
where an untanned teenager
leisurely accepts burning-
white ultraviolet light—
ignorant of danger buzzing
inches from left ankle —
reads *Lord of the Flies,*
below blue beyond.

MISTAKEN IDENTITY

I step softly in shallow grass wet with dew,
brown and green leaves glistening in the sun

like flickering tongues. I forget my new rubber
hose, panic on glancing a thin yellow stripe

along a black back, six feet long, coiled at my feet.
As though ancient arch-enemy

dares me to walk by, risk being
bitten, or beaten by absolute fear.

HUSH

Sudden summer thunderstorms
march across southern sky,
invading armies pushing aside
ballgames, equestrians jumping
over latticed fences, these placid
summer scenes turned quixotic.
Dark clouds dominate
landscapes, send crushing
cascading lightening, rain, hail.

Summertime living is not always easy,
despite jumping catfish, knee-high corn,
rich daddies and good looking mamas.

I hear chickadees, sparrows, early-mating wrens this morning when
I rise in the dark, move cautiously outside, gaze into the pre-dawn,
and look east for a sign that rain might be stored in some vast bin of
the horizon, near where stars, half-visible, still hang low.

My dog barks at a neighbor's cough. I let it pass. I'm still half-asleep,
not much for waving at a dimly-lit man. Better to keep hold of my
recent dreaming than spend it on tedious greetings.

Doubtless I am vain to think rain will fall now, before September
begins, before we forget summer's splendid, autumn's sublime.
Looking for rain, we grow unsociable. Without it, we have little
harvest.

I keep watch, wait.

AUGUST CLAMOR, QUIET

1.

Sunlight strains to stretch
through dry hydrangea
stalks, stems tall and upright,
composed, stately and serene.
A doe does not blink, nor tail flick
a fly, or eye my intrusion
into her morning snack,
her August ritual made more
faultless with sips of providential
bird bath water, rude needless
noises reverberating from a
cell phone nearby.

2.

Pasted to the pearly white ceiling
of the car port an ebon wasp—
isolate cum ever-present with
a constant barrage of buzzing,
saw-like sounds—enough to signal
cicadas exited to some faraway
destiny, leaving their shells to abide
the mud-daubers' nauseous mucus
membranes resonate in deaf ear drums
with its irritating noise, its pitiful
painful cacophony, blistering sting.

3.

Across the street, a Jack Russel yapper
begins its unceasing clamor before
the moon sets, the sun rises. Though ancients
proclaim dogs are faithful friends, this yapping
creature is obnoxious personified, barking his
fame. The wasp—
awake but noiseless now—still ferments
its spit, the doe amicably nurses
her fawn, while the sleeping mortal
dreams not of unicorns but of endless
winding brooks, forever lush ferns, happy
numbered sparrows tucked into scrap-
filled nests high in the Bradford Pear
tree foliage, safe from the viper's venom.
Neither Caesar nor Saint Augustus disturbs
the destiny of deer, wasps, rude dogs,
or peaceful people with beatific dreams.

—for Michael

MOCKINGBIRD, THE MORNING AFTER

My God, you are so loud and cheerful this early
after a night of torrential rain, hurricane winds,
limbs disconnected, broken, and strewn through the yard.
If not for rafters where your nest stayed tucked and dry,
you might have drowned, mockingbird,
after three days of raining straight.

You open your throat to sing as if a little boy has not
just drowned, or whole homes have not been swept away
by flood, or even as if the Bradford pear, once neatly kept,
isn't stripped bare, like its sister oaks and dogwoods nearby.

Is it natural in the great order for you to sing while I weep,
for you to be pert while I mourn, while you seem
heedless of my health, while my friends plan funerals?
You cock your head, tune up your voice one more time,
mock my loss, mock my pain, mock my weary world.

MOURNING

This winter morning, fumbling
with thin-skinned and fragile fingers
to touch familiar objects
placed carefully on the bedside chair.
I'm hugged, gently, by a robe, and
off-balance I sway, searching
unsuccessfully for slippers among
shadows offering pale succor
cast by night-light from the
nearby hall.
Unstable
feet inch forward,
dawn draws on relentlessly.
My wife of fifty years breathes unevenly
while our grandchild sleeps uneasily in
the plush bed upstairs. Loss filled
dreams displace restful nights, as
our will bends slowly toward some strange
and unfamiliar tomorrow. Dim blue
eyes long for light-filled days,
or to see something like
stars.

ON THE DEMISE OF A PYGMY MOUSE

You

Squinted

Meekly

Pondering

How to survive

Near the end

Of your

Short

Soggy life.

Lap dogs

Tread water

Without webbing

Black bugs

Stick thin

Appendages

Float

Like Olympians—

Smooth

Effort-

Less strokes

Eyes focused

On a lakeshore—

Else meet their

Fate like

You:

Wet

Fur

Floating

Near

The scum stain

On the side

Of a stainless steel

Kitchen sink.

IN WINTER

That first solstice,
now more than fifty winters gone,
newlywed, we shared cots
in an Army post guesthouse,
making myths
more urgently than
two might
in fantasy—or dramatic monologues.

Tonight,
we create new marrow
with bones grown old by age,
synaptic impulses guiding fingers,
arrhythmic hearts beating in synch,
hopes growing dim with too little
remembrance of years past.

As in our first winter,
we embrace
each other's desire
for the longest evening
never to end,
revel in ecstasies found
in hours together.

FELICITY

As if from some bleak dream, I awaken,
squint at red figures like soldiers,
held at attention on the bedside clock,
digits now blurred, like all the world,
after the blinding onset of macular degeneration.

A worm-tune loops endlessly between my ears,
        Carly Simon's *Let the River Run.* I consider if
   I also hear rain,
          or do I dream?

Insistent tapping of rain
on window panes fades:
   Kiri te Kanawa, solo,
   sings
   Night gathers round my soul.
      Listening, on the razor
      edge of sleep, I ease down under
      soft folds of well-worn quilt.
        Find fitful sleep,

O,   *divine*   *Redeemer.*

MUTABILITY

What's a soul to do, after all—
after the generous warmth
of loved ones, the thin balm
offered by restless voices?

A chill comes, not cruel,
only autumn's first breath—
mild sourness like a child's
banter turned bitter
post-laughter. Stabbing
ache beneath the ribs,
unsteady and painful heart,
uneasy rub where abides the spleen,
leaving little room for the warmth
of summer friends.

The mind's gray matter—calm, beautiful,
reassured—gathers itself for future losses,
leaves a clearing. Makes room
where grace abides.
The soul relieved,
accedes.

Out,   out, black'd   out   words
holy script   unholy deeds
un-   redacted   crimes

PERSPECTIVE

(Late tonight, almost tomorrow) I sit on my apartment balcony, watch stars barely blink, their little dying eyes dimmer each night I'm here—(Now), I see plane lights nosing toward giant satelites orbiting earth as gods would do. In this vast panoply I can almost forget turmoil roiling around our world: so many fires out west, so many glaciers melting, so many schools in terror, as my own little world swirls with news of aged friends passing away. Robert Frost's advice to *choose something like a star* to be *staid* seems sage. I'll sit out here under their glow until that great east star comes up across the way.

NOMENCLATURE

The first doctor I knew smelled of ripe
    pipe tobacco. I gagged when he
    asked me to say *ahhhhh*, pressing my tongue
    with a flat board resembling a wide popsicle stick.
    He tapped my teeth, peered into my throat, gave a few
    jolting grunts.

My doctor today *taps taps taps*
    on my chest, asks and waits for the *ahhhhh* as well.
    He pokes around my wrinkle maze, squints,
    at old spots or brown blemishes, finishing his tour
    with a stern sermon against my sins of diet.
    My singing heart beats a strong song while my
    old soul and body flutter *ahhhhhhh*.

—for FK

HYDRANGEA LIGHT

Study, thoughtfully,

age spots on your wrinkled

scabby arms, until,

closing your eyes,

turn your vision inward

and begin to see

pink and blue polka dots

which are not dots at all

but harbingers of an end

to those perfect days

when you were ten;

the sun set then as

now, and you were

certain it would rise

the next morning.

Today's sunset is four hours off,

already it lingers—

a sheen across the wilting

blue-and-pink hydrangeas

breathing late-summer air

long enough for you to catch

rivulets of light

strung between the dots.

DELTA PILGRIMAGE

That day we brought Dad home from Memphis
VA Hospital, the great Mississippi flood extended
farther than even we feared. Driving west across
the arching bridge into Arkansas we heard water
lap, lap, lapping against soaked shores and levees,
like giant dogs quenching their thirst for land.

Dad lay propped on pillows in the back seat
of mom's car, infected with the joy of traveling
toward home. He hoped to see once more his native
land, though most of it lay buried beneath a swollen tide.
Rinsed in tears, his ancient eyes surveyed low lying
lands where cotton, corn, soybeans, rice—
and catfish—should be growing. Instead

trailer tops, odd-shaped outhouses, lop-sided
utility poles, detritus from people and land
in Ohio, Kentucky, Missouri floated along near
levees high as the old earthworks once raised
by Chickasaw ancestors who lived here
centuries before. For more than
fifty miles we drove slowly, the water still
menacing as we slipped along moist asphalt.

On the radio, we heard *Shall We Gather at the River.*
Dad kept time by tapping softly on Mom's arm.
In a couple of hours at last we left behind the vast
watery Delta. To this day, I do not know how
bright angel feet have trod on water, as the song says.
Dad's smile at the end suggested he knew.

PEACE LIKE A RIVER

The boy dribbles a dusty brown ball,
walks slowly—shirt dark with sweat,
cap bent low, hands like a farmhand's.
His sister dawdles behind,
searching a pasture for clover,
both crossing toward friends.
The sun, an orange rim,
rests on the green tops of trees.

       Two soles stick up from the ground,
thin as dried jimson weeds
wavering in a March breeze.
The boy freezes,
then runs.

       The ball drops.

He falls,
gags as his stomach turns,
sour heat spilling from his mouth,
mucus and tears mingling,
despite his will,
as if taken by a fever—
He feels his small world split open
like the man's cut throat before him.

He knows those overalls,
patched and faded.
Knows the red cap.
                    Flies, yellow-jackets
          trace the cut
from ear to ear—
     a cruel, uneven smile.

His sister's hand finds
his shoulder.
They stare at the hands
that once threw fastballs
past the summer dusk.
                         The girl leaves
to bring their mother.

He pulls his shirt free,
          rips it down the middle,
lays it across the old man's chest,
straightens the cap,
and sits on the ball,

          bare in the failing light

When Mama arrives, doves
note the sunset, she asks
Honey, why are you naked?
Finds her young son,
oldened, bereft
beside his ball

       the field gone still.

RADIO BASEBALL

Almost any poet who has made music worth hearing
has tried a baseball poem.
Unfortunately, Mighty Casey is not alone in striking out.
Bad poems and baseball

inflict more heartbreak than unrequited love,
offer more metaphors for life's
lessons than Polonius. I wanted to write my ode
to the changeup or the slider,

but kept postponing it—
felt like a rookie somewhere in the minors,
warming up in the bullpen
for a team without a name. I dreamed of writing that poem

early on because memory fails,
but teenage angst and echoes of the
Cards against the Cubs deep into the night
kept fading like an eighth-inning fastball,

details more elusive than a Niekro knuckler.
And each time I thought of a poem,
something about you intervened.
What was it? Baseball poems are about boys

and dads playing catch and yelling,
Slide, dammit, slide!
But I recall few moments with you and me and the game,
except those we shared listening to the radio.

I was out to prove bonds
between shagging baseballs and dreams.
I should have known my memory
had already been fed forever by radio baseball

with you. Still, something
about recreating the game with you
made me want to shape those moments
into a poem, but

The only gift you gave me
was your love of the game.
You did not throw catch with me
or take me out to a ballpark.

I never saw you argue with an ump.
You never saw me slide safely home.
You went away and never returned
except in my dreams.

Before you left we did turn on the radio.
We heard Harry Caray.
Years later when I saw you,
I was past puberty but a baseball fan for life.

We didn't talk at all.
I couldn't tell
if you still loved the game—
or me.

ADDING UP THE LOSSES

In the small tract of land
behind our house where we've lived long enough
to raise grandchildren, developers finally found
the right price to entice owners to sell.
Today, we added up our losses.

A staggering number of
nature's perennials: tall hardwoods and pines,
sumac, dogwood, squirrels, generations of ticks,
Canada geese, rabbits, raccoons, deer, owls singing preludes to
poems written before dawn, millions of chiggers

Cardinals, Blue Birds, Woodpeckers, Finches both
Purple and Yellow, Carolina Wrens, dandelion,
blackberries, wild strawberries, mice, rats, copperheads and
common garden snakes, happy Sparrows, Chickadees,

and our children's woods where they waded in the streams
and fished the pond, reveled as if they owned the land themselves.

Oh, and this: two turkeys are with-
out a home. We spotted them this week when the
tractors and trucks came to cut and haul the trees, rearrange the
land for condos, chase Carolina's critters away

We and all the creatures seem to be

adjusting except for the turkeys:

Today, they stood in the

       middle of a busy road,

confused,   unhappy,   *lost.*

DECOMPOSITION

I am elbow-deep
in a bag of dirt
I bought today
at a back-road hardware store.

Dark soil, enhanced
to pump iron and life
into potted parsley,
freesia, shoots of groundcover.

This dirt's rich enough
to grow a patch of diamonds,
fifty pounds of pure essence,
like that used for molding Adam,

or composting Walt Whitman,
both my hands
full, celebrating Spring
deep underneath
jagged
fingernails.

HALLOWED

Rough and heartless late October winds
blow and blow today, havoc for fireflies
and lady bugs who may have buzzed
about the rapture arriving early in bugland.
The gleaming golden maple in your yard—
its corner claimed decades ago—shed
layers of leaf showers. A few stingy,
broken limbs litter, yet cannot dim
a thick yellow carpet among pine straw
needle clusters. Out walking, wondering
what to make of this serendipity, aged
folks, timid teens, mamas on cell phones
pause while on the scene a hallowed landscape artist
breathes *hold it right there.*

—for Frances (Weenie) and William (Bill)

LOVE IN HURRICANE SEASON

And I will watch the spindly pine
trees shrug and quiver when the thrust
of wild wind one hundred miles per hour
slashes across our back orchard and beyond.

And I will speak softly, calmly to you, hold
my heart, your hand if necessary when
the thunder rolls, the bolts of blue skies slice
across our soggy zoysia grass, greening.

And I will never let you go again until
the next hurricane, whether this year
or a century from now, when you and
I and all that's ours takes us safely home.

BEFORE DAWN

Who knows what's going on in the brain before dawn,
when I rise to read the morning paper, drawn

to the backyard to see the moon display its last rays
on frosted grass, shine its grace on an owl

hooting the last stanzas of some ever-ongoing poem.
At the feeder, small wings quarrel for sweet water—

butterfly, bee, gnat, small engines of desire.
Somewhere near, a voice once caged

rises to join the chorus—Sappho, Sexton, Wheatley,
Plath, Bradstreet, Dickinson, Clifton, Kenyon, Lazarus,

Homer, Eliot, Frost, Angelou, Lowell, Whitman, Hughes—
an abridged list of notables so long I can only imagine

each of them singing the same astonishing
melodies in chorus with one another,

and suddenly I am a teenager again,
as if seven and more decades have not passed,

the same moon still in its youth,
the same mind, still composing.

LOBLOLLY PRESS

Loblolly Press is an independent press based out of Asheville, North Carolina that is dedicated to publishing contemporary poetry, short fiction, and novels from emerging and marginalized writers across the American South. Our goal is to publish writers with a distinctly Southern voice from communities and experiences not always represented in traditional publishing. We're striving to create a community of writers and readers who feel deeply connected to the work we publish because they can see themselves represented within it.

RECENT AND FORTHCOMING FROM LOBLOLLY PRESS

The Surfacing of Joy   Earl J. Wilcox (2023)

If Lost   Clint Bowman (2024)

Distant Relations   Cheryl Whitehead (2025)

Beasts of Chase   Andrew Mack (2025)

The Computer Room   Emma Ensley (2025)

Proud Roads   Kelly Riedesel (2025)

Habitats   Garrett Ashley (2026)

Titles set in Acumin Pro. Text set in Cormorant.

www.ingramcontent.com/pod-product-compliance
Lightning Source LLC
Chambersburg PA
CBHW040914010826
48978CB00013BB/1286